newsmallhomes

newsmallhomes

Editor: Aurora Cuito

Text: Aurora Cuito, Mario Catelli (*Subtle Distribution*)

Translation: Bill Bain, Julie King

Proofreading: Julie King

Art director: Mireia Casanovas Soley

Graphic design: Emma Termes Parera

Illustrations: Marco Roso and Horacio Polanco

chergburgo@hotmail.com

2001 © Loft Publications s.l.

ISBN Softcover: 0-8230-3195-0

D.L.: B-51.455-2000

Printed in Spain
Gràfiques Ibèria S.A.

2001 © Loft Publications S.L. and HBI,
an imprint of HarperCollins Publishers

First published in 2001 by LOFT and HBI,
an imprint of HarperCollins Publishers
10 East 53rd St. New York, NY 10022-5299

Distributed in the U.S. and Canada by Watson-Guptill Publications
770 Broadway New York, NY 10003-9595
Telephone: (800) 451-1741 or (732) 363-4511 in NJ, AK, HI Fax: (732) 363-0338

Distributed throughout the rest of the world by
HarperCollins International
10 East 53rd St. New York, NY 10022-5299
Fax: (212) 207-7654

If you would like to suggest projects for inclusion in our next volumes,
please e-mail details to us at: loft@loftpublications.com

We have tried our best to contact all copyright holders.
In individual cases where this has not been possible,
we request copyright holders to get in touch with the publishing house.

Pool Architektur	16	LIVING IN A WATER TANK	194 sq. feet
Kaufmann & Kaufmann	22	THE FRED PROTOTYPE	194 sq. feet
Kaufmann & Kaufmann	28	SU-SI PROTOTYPE	322 sq. feet
Flores and Prats, Duch and Pizà	36	PORTMANTEAU	430 sq. feet
Ivan Kroupa	42	LIVING IN A CONTAINER	480 sq. feet
Joseph Giovannini Associates	48	VOLUMETRIC CHAOS	535 sq. feet
William Smart Architects	54	FUNCTIONAL VARIABILITY	538 sq. feet
Eichinger oder Knechtl	60	GLASS BOX ATTIC	560 sq. feet
Cecconi Simone Inc.	68	NAUTICAL LOFT	623 sq. feet
Claesson Koivisto Rune Arkitektkontor	74	A TRANQUIL OASIS	700 sq. feet
Simon Platt and Rob Dubois	78	POLYVALENT APARTMENT	750 sq. feet
Claesson Koivisto Rune Arkitektkontor	84	ORGANIC SPACES	763 sq. feet
Madinabeitia and Barrio	92	SUBTLE DISTRIBUTION	850 sq. feet
A-cero Arquitectos	98	DIAPHANOUS CONTINUTY	860 sq. feet
Haehndel and Coll	106	A REFORMED STABLE	860 sq. feet
Olli Sarlin and Marja Sopanen	112	INDUSTRIAL PÀST	915 sq. feet
Cecconi Simone Inc.	118	INDUSTRIAL LOFT	915 sq. feet
W. Camagna, M. Camoletto and A. Marcante	122	TRANSLUCENT STAIRCASE	960 sq. feet
Marco Savorelli	128	MINIMALIST ATTIC APATMENT	960 sq. feet
Christophe Pillet	136	LUMINOUS CONTINUITY	960 sq. feet
Voon Wong	142	FLOATING ISLAND	960 sq. feet
Satoshi Okada	150	SPIRAL STRIP	970 sq. feet
John Cockings Architects	156	TRANSLUCENT COLOR	975 sq. feet
Atelier Suda	162	3-D EXPANSION	980 sq. feet
Claudio Lazzarini & Carl Pickering	166	LUMINOUS WALL	1,000 sq. feet

Introduction

This book presents a selection of apartments, single-family homes and lofts that have managed to create a spacious atmosphere in less than 1,000 square feet. The homes were chosen because they offer practical solutions to problems derived from a lack of space.

New Small Homes contains a wealth of ideas on how to make a small home more comfortable. One solution is to use partition walls on wheels, moveable closets or sliding doors that enable the residents to alter the distribution of the rooms according to their needs. Another ingenious strategy is to take advantage of empty corners by installing folding tables or custom-built shelves and closets.

Some architects use a home's vertical space to create a new level. Lofts caneasily accommodate a studio, an extra bedroom or storage. Furnishings also play an important role since their careful selection can make a home appear larger than it is. Architects have specially designed some of the multi-purpose furnishings included in these pages.

In the introduction, we wanted to highlight the most brilliant resources. Constructive elements like windows, skylights and stairs can distort the perception of space. Special strategies in kitchens and bathrooms can make them more practical. And optional elements, like terraces, attics and furnishings, can optimize the small interior of a home.

windows

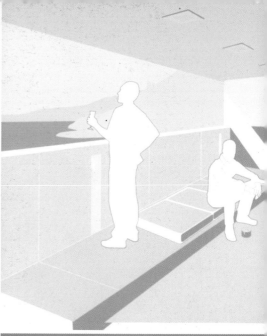

The strategic installation of windows permits abundant light to enter the residence in a way that makes the space seem larger than it is. Poor lighting can cause the house to appear smaller. Openings in vertical partitions can link distinct rooms and generate a continuity that gives the project the feeling of a large, connected space, not just the sum of many small rooms.

terraces

Terraces are elements that bring value to the residence, not only for the luxury of dining outdoors on a hot day, but because they increase the area of a house, even if only in a perceptive way. Glass façades establish a direct relationship between the interior and the exterior, so that even while indoors, the terrace, the views, the city and the sky form part of the home.

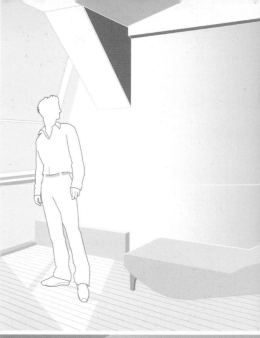

skylights

Many of the lofts presented in the book are blessed with skylights that respond to the ceiling's reduced dimensions, whether low or sloped. Skylights break up the roof and lighten it. Views of the sky and natural light add warmth to the atmosphere.

stairs

The staircases that appear in the book have been designed to take up the minimal amount of space. For this reason, most of them are not limited by walls, some are pushed up against the wall. Others feature glass steps through which light can pass in order not to interrupt the space. In addition to linking various levels, some staircases take advantage of the space below for closets or drawers.

closets

Closets play a fundamental role in small homes because they accommodate distinct functions. In the projects described, we find large pieces of furniture containing bathrooms, kitchens or beds that can close to conceal their function. In other cases, we find mobile closets that can slide to reorganize a room or that can hide in the wall and disappear.

attics

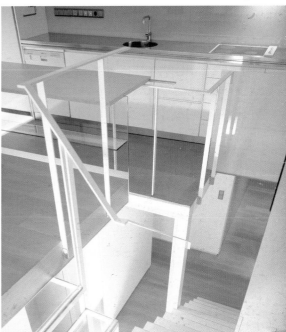

Though all the projects share the quality of a small surface area, some of them enjoy high ceilings. In these cases, the architects have taken advantage of the height to create distinct levels inside one domestic space. In most of the examples, the attic is visually related to the main floor by way of glass partitions or medium-height partition walls that create continuity in order to increase the sensation of space.

kitchens

The reduced dimensions of the homes included in this book required that most elements be specially designed for each case. Since it is often impossible to find kitchens for such limited measurements, the architects had to create imaginative solutions. Some kitchens are located inside pieces of furniture that can be closed. Others occupy only a bar, and many of them are open to the living room or the dining room.

bathrooms

The small bathrooms were designed using ingenious and experimental construction solutions. In some cases, the bathroom forms part of the room, and in others — especially in those that do not require privacy — they have been placed in the middle of the living room. The materials used are not always conventional tiles. The designers have also incorporated new components like metallic mesh, stainless steel and, even, wood.

LIVING IN A WATER TANK
Pool Architektur

THIS project is located on the terrace of an old industrial building in Vienna that was restored to house offices and workshops. Pool Architektur, a young and daring Austrian team, managed to transform the building's water tank into a micro-apartment. The result is an example of how a true home can be created in only 194 square feet.

Even though the tank no longer contains water, the architects preserved its original structure, including the sloping walls on the lower part. Though they painted the brick white, they did not smooth it out or rejoin it in order to maintain its rough texture. The glass façade that leads onto the terrace provides the apartment with views of the city's rooftops.

Most of the furniture, including the bed, the dining table and the closet, is mobile and slides into a small metal volume in the wall when not in use. This storage volume sticks out of the construction and enables the residents to free up space inside.

The kitchen projects out of the wall and is a sculptural element made of a metal sheet in the form of an L. The refrigerator is suspended from the ceiling and is strategically positioned to facilitate its use without blocking the passageway.

The shower consists of a metallic plate and a faucet inserted into the wall. The architects did not hang curtains because the one space that requires privacy, the bathroom, is closed off. A rotating television sits in a nook in the wall and can be turned towards either the bathroom or the living room.

Pool Architektur has demonstrated that claustrophobia does not result from a home's measurements, but from poor management of space.

Architects: Pool Architektur **Photographs:** Hertha Hurnaus **Location:** Vienna, Austria **Completion date:** 1999 **Area:** 194 sq. feet

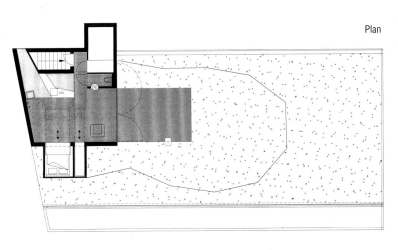

Plan

PREVIOUS PAGE. Images of the various furniture pieces that can be moved to create distinct spaces. The only moveable pieces are the sofa and a lamp.

LEFT. A television on a rotating metallic platform is inserted into the wall and can be turned either towards the bathroom or towards the living area and the bedroom.

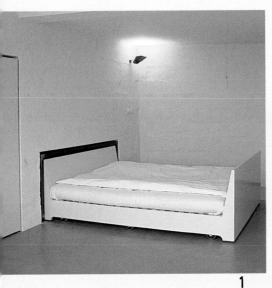

1   2   3

DESIGN SOLUTIONS

1. The furniture slides towards the exterior when not in use. This mobility enables the residence to be more spacious during the day, when the bed and closet are stored in the metallic volume that protects them from the harsh weather.

2. The glass façade permits an intense relationship between the interior and the exterior by widening the resident's perception of space.

3. The kitchen furniture juts out of the wall but does not touch the floor. The refrigerator is suspended from the ceiling so that no object interrupts the apartment's small surface area.

THE FRED PROTOTYPE
Kaufmann & Kaufmann

THE Fred prototype is a prefabricated residence formed by a 99 x 99 x 99 foot cube that can be enlarged by means of a module that slides along rails using an electronic mechanism. The designers, an Austrian team formed by the brothers Oskar Leo and Johannes Kaufmann, dreamed up a house that—despite its reduced dimensions—can accommodate the domestic necessities of every home: a complete kitchen, a bathroom and an area that can be used as a bedroom or a living area.

A top priority was the home's mobility: to be able to construct it easily on distinct lots. To achieve this objective, the designers created a project that is transportable by truck and that needs only the help of a crane to set it on the ground. Since the module would be moved, the construction had to be strong enough that it would not fall apart. The Kaufmann brothers used high quality materials and closely supervised the production process.

Once Fred was placed on a lot, the client could extend it using the electronic system and connect it to the sewage system and electrical network. When moving the house, the furnishings items, including chairs and other pieces, can be secured and transported inside the module.

The architects chose wood for the roof, and glass and wood for the façades. The walls feature an efficient insulation system that conserves the energy that passes through the glass.

In short, Fred is a carefully designed prefabricated home that is both functional and aesthetically pleasing.

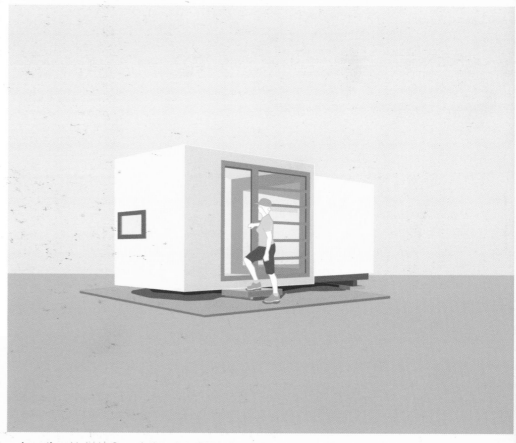

Architects: Kaufmann & Kaufmann **Photographs:** Ignacio Martínez **Location:** Variable **Completion date:** 1999 **Area:** 194-624 sq. feet

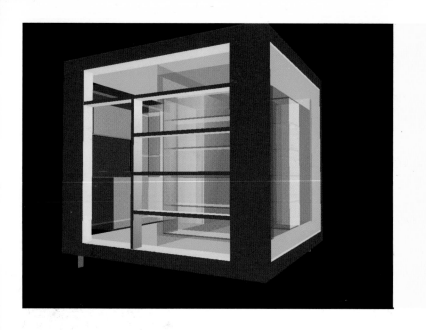

THIS PAGE. The diagrams present the prototype and the various ways it can be used. The perspectives demonstrate how the module can be adapted to uneven terrain using a system of pillars that lift it off the ground and regulate its height so that the floor remains in a horizontal position.

Perspectives

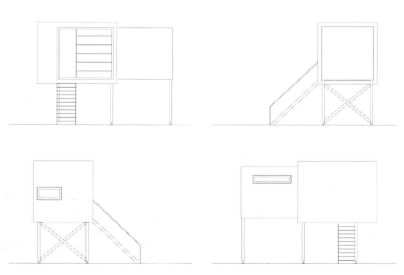

Elevations

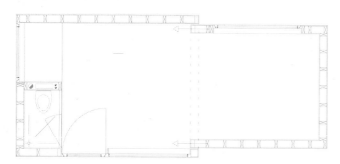

Floor plan when expanded

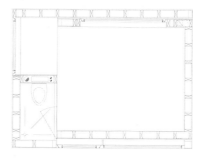

Floor plan when closed

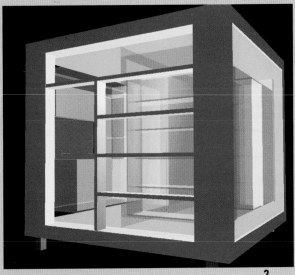

1

2

3

DESIGN SOLUTIONS

1. Prefabricated homes are the result of a meticulous functional study that takes maximum advantage of space. Every part has a precise place and measurement. The benefit of Fred is that it offers a certain amount of flexibility in terms of how it can be used.

2. Computer simulations show the prototype's various distribution possibilities. Fred can be treated as a day pavilion or as the guestroom of a house with a garden.

3. The selected materials and construction techniques make it fast and inexpensive to set up the prototype, and simple to move it.

SU-SI PROTOTYPE
Kaufmann & Kaufmann

THIS prefabricated residence evolved from studies that Kaufmann & Kaufmann conducted to respond to today's functional and aesthetic requirements. As an alternative to the conventional construction built on a single plot of land, they have created a mobile structural unit that can easily be set up or transported from one location to another, without sacrificing a warm domestic environment.

The architecture behind this prefabricated dwelling is innovative and has nothing to do with the old cabins that were constructed as emergency solutions. Su-si can accommodate a comfortable residence with all the latest technological advances, including electrical appliances and installations. Once set on the ground, it can easily be connected to the sewage system and electrical network.

The house is made of wood and glass. Insulation was carefully distributed to block the inclement weather of Austria, the country in which the residence was first built. There are no openings on the lateral façades, but the upper part of the back façade, meant to be placed towards the north, does feature an elongated window. This glass façade was designed to capture natural light and runs along the dining room, living room and the bedroom, which is separated from the house by an armoire.

Since the project is normally built upon request, the architects can alter various parts according to the wishes of each client. The prototype can be used for residential purposes (as a home for one or two people, as a guest house or a second residence), or for commercial ends (as an exhibition hall, studio or construction office).

The quality and excellence of Su-si has been recognized with two prestigious Austrian design awards: the IF Design Award and the Holzbaupreis.

Architects: Kaufmann & Kaufmann **Photographs:** Ignacio Martínez **Location:** Variable **Completion date:** 1999 **Area:** 323-538 sq. feet

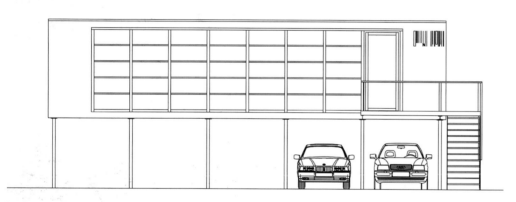

Elevation

TOP. The Kaufmann brothers come from a family of carpenters and have extensive experience with wood constructions. Their knowledge of carpentry enables them to create prototypes that respond perfectly to structural and functional demands.

NEXT PAGE. With just a few workers, the prototype can be set up in five hours. The module is transported by truck to the building site where a crane places it on top of pillars that level the ground.

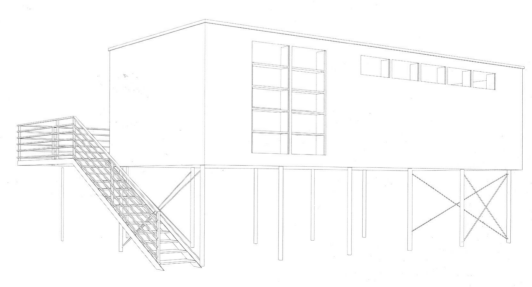

Axonometric perspective

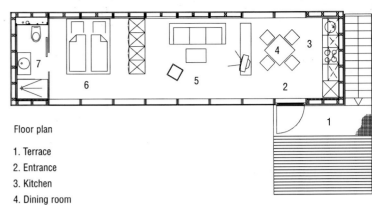

Floor plan

1. Terrace
2. Entrance
3. Kitchen
4. Dining room
5. Living room
6. Bedroom
7. Bathroom

TOP. With such a limited floor plan, there are few distribution alternatives. The Austrian architects have positioned the kitchen and the bathroom on the outer edges so that the central space can be distributed according to the client's needs. Possibilities include a large living room and a bedroom, two bedrooms, or a dining room, a living area and a bed.

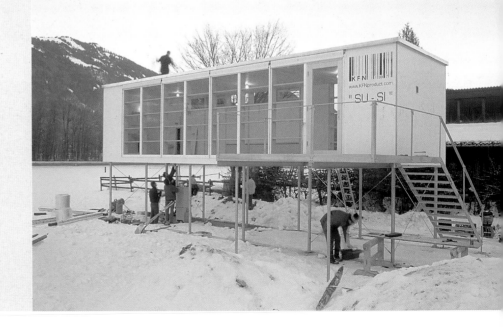

1 **2** **3**

DESIGN SOLUTIONS

1. The house is built in a workshop to allow for more precise attention to detail. Production takes five weeks and the house can be set up in only five hours, making it much less expensive than a conventional residence.

2. One of the façades of the Su-si prototype is all glass, which provides views of the surroundings and amplifies the project's virtual area. The landscape becomes an integral part of the domestic space.

3. The kitchen and the bathroom are located on the building's extremes in order to free up the central area, which does not require water installations.

PORTMANTEAU
Flores and Prats, Duch and Pizà

THE idea arose from the clients' need for a town house in Barcelona. They live on the island of Majorca and travel to the city once or twice a month. A tiny condominium that was practical and conveniently located would answer their needs. They found just the spot in Barcelona's Ensanche neighborhood and commissioned the building of a small attic.

Their aims were well-defined: a luminous space that would be easy to clean, with almost no maintenance requirements and a warm feel to it even if it remained empty most of the time.

The architects compared its use to one of those enormous trunks used by travelers in former times: on reaching your destination, you opened it and it became a container to hold all your basic needs. Basing their drawings on this idea, the architects came up with two large wood-lined modules for all the functions of the house. Opening each part would reveal the different concealed uses that fragment the dwelling into the minimal spaces each activity requires.

The furniture is arranged to suit the demands of the spur of the moment. The single, unified space of the two rooms varies according to the use required. One room contains a bed, two queen-size closets, an armchair, and a jewel box; the other has a single bed, a stove, a refrigerator, a pantry, and a table.

The lighting comes from a long skylight that runs the full 25 1/2 foot length of the dwelling. Like a crack of light it is only interrupted by the metal beams that hold up the roof. The entire house was painted white to increase luminosity and contrast with the tones of the wooden furniture and parquet.

Before departing, the owners close up their portmanteau and leave the space ordered and well-lit till next visit.

Architects: Flores and Prats, Duch and Pizà **Photographs:** Eugeni Pons **Location:** Barcelona, Spain **Completion date:** 1997 **Area:** 430 sq. feet

TOP. The clients only spend a few days a month in this apartment and want no frills. All the utensils in the kitchen and bath can be easily stored in the cabinets.

BOTTOM. The section shows the arrangement of the attic in relation to the building's façade. It was necessary to set the structure away from the front since the Ensanche neighborhood's building code allows height increase only if the addition is not visible from the street.

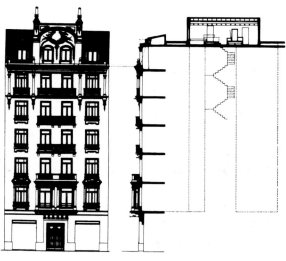

Elevation and section of the building

TOP. The bed folds into one of the closets. This mechanism has two advantages: there is greater floor space during the day, and when the apartment is closed, the mattress simply slides away for storage.

BOTTOM. The cabinet containing the stove opens to reveal the refrigerator and a dining table held up by a wooden bracket.

a. Floor plan
b. Cross section
c. Transverse section

1. Bathroom
2. Foldout bed
3. Kitchen
4. Bed
5. Equipment

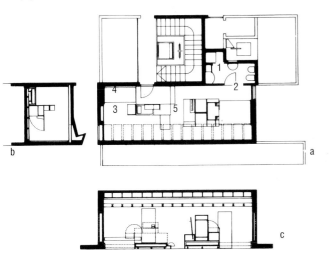

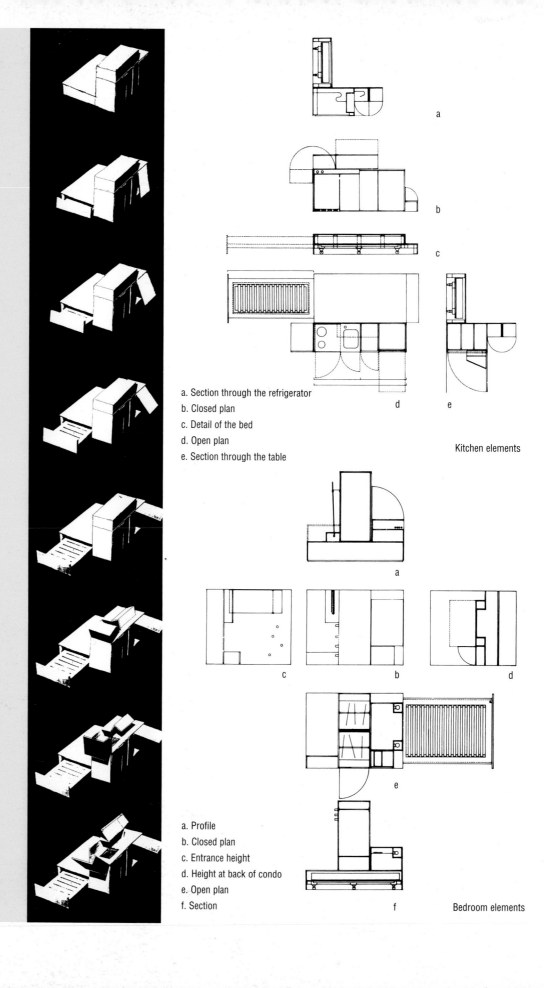

LEFT. The strip of drawings shows how the wooden furniture folds up to leave a functional configuration. Originally, only some of the shelves opened out, but the clients now enjoy all the features of a conventional dwelling.

RIGHT. These plans decode the internal framing of the furniture, custom-designed to save space. Special attention was paid to making the parts light and mobile so that the elements could be changed easily and quickly.

a. Section through the refrigerator
b. Closed plan
c. Detail of the bed
d. Open plan
e. Section through the table

Kitchen elements

a. Profile
b. Closed plan
c. Entrance height
d. Height at back of condo
e. Open plan
f. Section

Bedroom elements

1

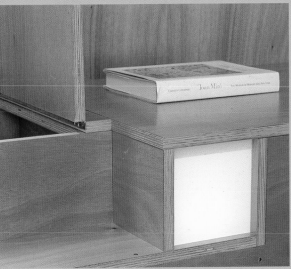

2

3

DESIGN SOLUTIONS

1. Two rooms were designed to contain all the domestic functions. While the clients are away from the condo, these elements can be closed to keep the contents clean and to eliminate the need for a dust cover.

2. The offset of the wooden furniture in some corners frees up space for shelves or lighting.

3. Homogeneous, natural lighting comes through a narrow sky-light that runs the length of the apartment. The light rays are interrupted only by the frame's metal beams.

RESIDENCE IN A CONTAINER

Ivan Kroupa

THIS wooden house is located in a luxurious garden in Mukarov, a small town south of Prague. The design process was conditioned by a limited budget and by the requirements of the clients. The construction had to accommodate a guest room, a studio and a room for the children, plus a conventional residence. While the assignment did not have a specific program, it did entail creating a design that would be flexible enough to accommodate the various domestic functions.

The architect prioritized the relationship with the garden by creating a large terrace that acts as an intermediate space and that expands the perception of the interior. During the summer, it becomes part of the residence itself. To emphasize the indoor-outdoor connection, the designers used a glass façade that can be fully opened. However, to ensure security and thermal insulation, they designed blind walls that can be closed completely and that hide the windows.

The interior is characterized by its flexibility: one of the façades houses a polyvalent cabinet that contains the bed, the dressing room, the kitchen and closets of various sizes. Thus, all these spaces are united in one axis of the residence and a large room remains free so that the dining room, sofas and office can be set up without restrictions.

The entire house is made of wood. The wood floor has been varnished and the wooden furnishings have been painted and lacquered. The façades incorporate thermal insulation, and have been recovered on the northern side with metal plates that also shield the roof.

Architect: Ivan Kroupa **Photographs:** Matteo Piazza **Location:** Mukarov, Czech Republic **Completion date:** 1998 **Area:** 480 sq. feet

THIS PAGE. While the owners wanted to enjoy views of the countryside from the home´s interior, they also wanted to guarantee that the residence would be secure when they are away. As a solution, the architect created a closed container that can be opened by means of sliding façades and wood windows.

THIS PAGE. With the exception of a few small openings, the main façades are blind. One houses the entry and the other contains the closets, the bed and the kitchen, which can be closed off with a sliding door that also acts as a façade.

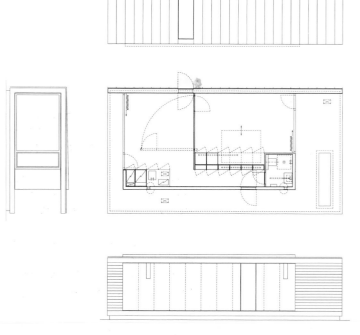

Plan and elevation.

1   2   3

DESIGN SOLUTIONS

1. Since the residence is located on an isolated lot, one of the main objectives was to guarantee the home's security when empty. The architect created exterior walls that are impenetrable when closed.

2. The kitchen is located in one of the cabinets in the entryway. Since all the cabinets have the same finish, the kitchen almost goes unnoticed and remains out of the way when not in use.

3. The lateral face consists of a glass façade and a running door made of painted wood. It serves three functions: to completely close the house, to permit the entry of light and views, and to separate the kitchen from the rest of the residence.

VOLUMETRIC CHAOS
Joseph Giovannini Associates

RESIDENTIAL architecture ordinarily tries to tame disorder, to clarify spaces and to offer calm in the face of frantic modern life. In this case, Joseph Giovannini designed a dwelling based on volumetric chaos that ended up shaping the project and creating the final result. The project entailed building a home in a constricted area that resisted compartmentalization. The architect had to struggle against the walls, which bend and angle in self-defense. The outcome is an apartment with a disordered composition of oblique planes and floating masses.

The final distribution, which hides a totally Cartesian past, responds to no fixed rules: cabinetry and shelving fill space in an anarchic way. The resulting structure is made up of wooden panels and sheets of metal, and was designed to tease out any number of perspectives. In addition, trompe l'oeil effects visually expand the apartment.

Upon entry, the viewer perceives the confusion of flat surfaces and partitions that disguise the traditional domestic functions: the kitchen, the cabinets, the bathroom, the bedroom and a small office. Like the majority of the rooms, the library floats on the surface of a partition, provoking a sense of loss of gravity that insights confusion but dilutes the spatial conflict.

The flooring, originally of marble, was replaced by wood in most of the house. The unpolluted facings are emphasized by a subtly concealed lighting system that sneaks out of nooks and crannies from behind the cabinets.

Architects: Joseph Giovannini Associates **Photographs:** Michael Moran **Location:** New York, US **Completion date:** 1999 **Area:** 535 sq. feet

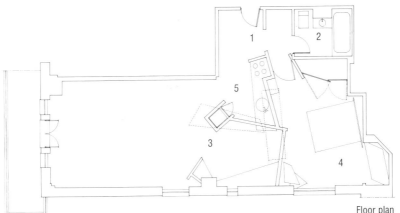
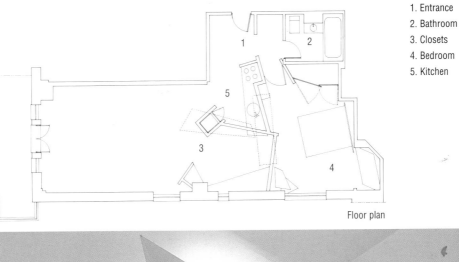

1. Entrance
2. Bathroom
3. Closets
4. Bedroom
5. Kitchen

Floor plan

TOP. Some of the masses hang from the ceiling, intersecting the beams that establish the structural order.

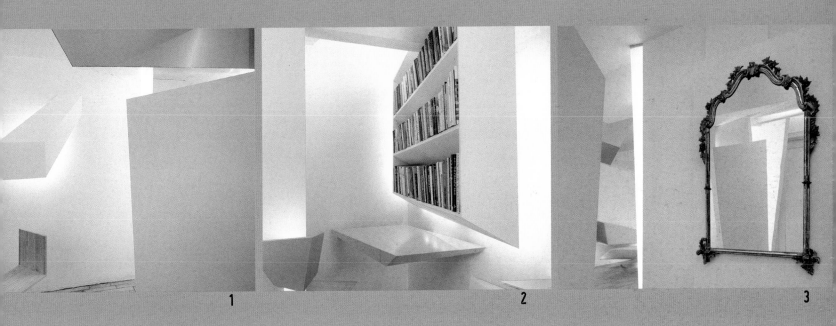

1   2   3

DESIGN SOLUTIONS

1. The chaotic distribution of plaster elements and of wood-and-metal cabinets provokes confusion to the senses. The planes arranged in all different directions trick the eye and increase the feeling of space.

2. Floating rooms like the library seem to defy gravity. They are so ethereal as to appear not to occupy any tangible space. The imprecise feeling that they are pieces on the point of disappearing helps optically widen the rooms.

3. Putting mirrors in small rooms is one of the oldest and most widely used strategies to increase the perception of space: they produce the obvious illusion of doubling the area.

FUNCTIONAL VARIABILITY
William Smart Architects

THE layout of this apartment, located on Australia's famous Bondi Beach, is organized around a dining table that pivots. The table rotates 180 degrees from the kitchen, past the studio and to the living room. It turns around a column that replaced the original structural wall. The structural system, made of stainless steel, supports a glass plate that is ten feet long and weighs 220 pounds.

To facilitate the table's movement, the work zone can be closed off with sliding fabric panels that offer privacy, yet are easily opened. The bedroom also has sliding doors made of translucent, bluish resin, which enable the residents to enjoy views of the sea from the bed. An electronically activated video projection ensures darkness at night by blocking the light that passes through the translucent panels.

The materials used in the apartment differ in luminosity and translucency in order to emphasize the impact of the views. The shiny finishes of the floor and table introduce the colors of the sky and sea inside the residence. Since there is hardly any frontier between the interior and the exterior spaces, seasonal and climactic changes dominate the apartment's character.

Though this home includes a complete music system, more than 60 points of light and the latest in television and video technology, the atmosphere is peaceful thanks to the careful design of the installations. A good example of the architects' skill for details is the large piece of white furniture that stores all the kitchen appliances and electronic apparatus, leaving the living room free of objects.

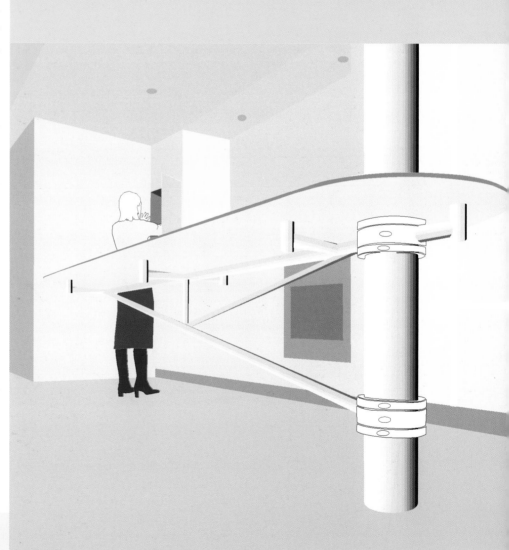

Architect: William Smart Architects **Photographs:** Gene Raymond Ross **Location:** Sydney, Australia **Construction date:**1999 **Area:** 538 square feet

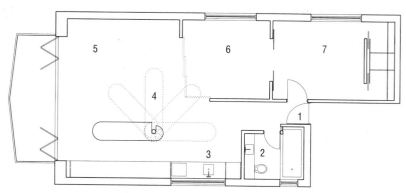

1. Entry
2. Bathroom
3. Kitchen
4. Dining room
5. Living room
6. Studio
7. Bedroom

1   2   3

DESIGN SOLUTIONS

1. The architects meticulously designed the construction system of the dining room table. The glass plate rotates within a range of 180 degrees.

2. Sliding doors and openings in the vertical partitions connect the spaces yet provide privacy when necessary.

3. Openings in the walls link the spaces and enable the studio and the bedroom to enjoy magnificent views of Bondi Beach.

GLASS BOX ATTIC
Eichinger oder Knechtl

AN old laundry that previously occupied the attic of a building was converted into a 560 square foot apartment with all the private spaces contained in a mere 344 square feet.

Existing partitions were removed and the ceiling beams were carefully covered with sheet metal. An exterior wall was then replaced by a large folding glass window.

Inside the home and behind a heavy, reinforced door is a wire mesh covering that integrates the cabinets and partitions off the spaces. The covering becomes a large lamp when lit at night. Inside the space are a washing machine and the control panel that is used to operate the windows, the lighting and the heating. This system of working the installations can also be operated by telephone.

When the stainless steel bathroom door is closed, a passageway leading to the back of the house becomes accessible. There we find the kitchen, an oak-lined area that leads outside where there is a small, decorative concrete planter filled with green plants. In the middle of the kitchen, a curtain unfolds to allow entry into a snow or rainwater shower beneath a skylight. Behind the kitchen, in the façade, the architects installed a glass cube that houses the toilet, which has views of the exterior.

The big window opens by means of a novel electric mechanism and consists of two parts: the upper piece can be raised up to 6 1/2 feet high, and the wall below the sill can extend the length of the kitchen to form a balcony and provide more living space.

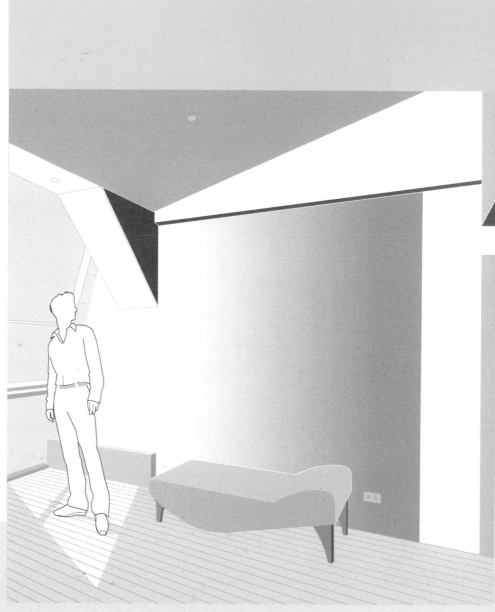

Architects: Eichinger oder Knechtl **Photographs:** Margherita Spiluttini **Location:** Vienna, Austria **Completion date:** 1998 **Area:** 560 sq. feet

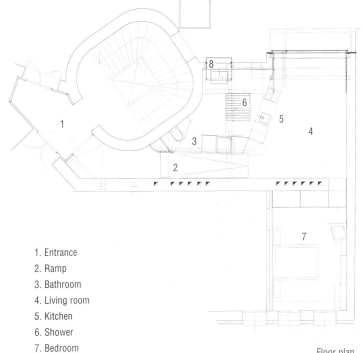

1. Entrance
2. Ramp
3. Bathroom
4. Living room
5. Kitchen
6. Shower
7. Bedroom
8. Toilet

Floor plan

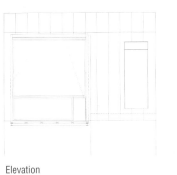

Elevation

Sections

PREVIOUS PAGE. View of the attic from the outside. The window is operated by two electric motors that make it possible to raise the large piece of glass as much as 6.5 feet.

THIS PAGE. The plans show the astute distribution of space. These young Austrian architects found mechanisms that maximize the dwelling's limited space.

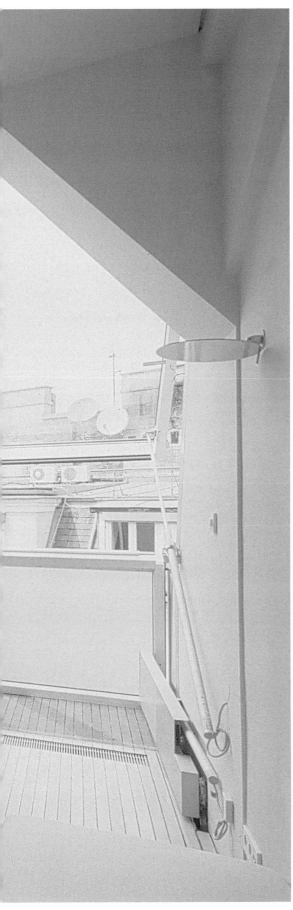

THIS PAGE. The kitchen includes an oak dresser fitted with cabinets and a sink.

LEFT. General view of the attic, wich enjoys abundant natural light flows and views of the city's rooftops. Electric lighting is controlled by a mechanism that can also be operated by telephone.

RIGHT. The wire mesh screen serves as a divider to partition off different spaces, and defines the bathroom and the shower. Above the shower is a skylight that drops rainwater for bathing and offers views of the night sky.

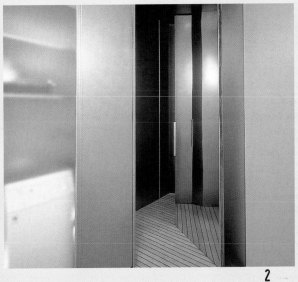
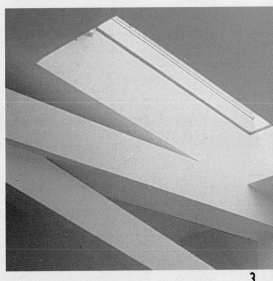

1

2

3

DESIGN SOLUTIONS

1. Vertical partitions were avoided throughout the dwelling except in the bedroom, which may be closed. The kitchen, for example, is open to the rest of the house and has a direct relation to the living room and the bathroom.

2. To increase the amount of light, even the small corners employ translucent materials (like the closet doors) or light-reflecting metals (as in the entranceway).

3. The skylight window above the shower gives a sense of openness. It is a small mechanism that enriches space perception and increases the amount of natural light.

NAUTICAL LOFT
Cecconi Simone Inc.

THIS project is the smallest of three model apartments that were created for the restoration of an old warehouse in downtown Toronto. The design of the loft was a challenge for the Cecconi Simone team since the space was both small and elongated.

The container's form is reminiscent of naval constructions, and some design elements were inspired by the nautical theme, such as curtains made out of sails, boat lights and metallic stairs.

Another objective was to convey the spirit of the original building. The space conserves the authentic columns and the exposed steel ceiling. Only the floor was sanded down in the kitchen and covered with wood in the sleeping area.

This home is the imaginative result of a study of the most effective use of space. The result features daring, aesthetic elements and ingenious tactics. Since there was so little surface area available, the designers optimized the apartment's height by creating distinct levels. They used the inside of the platforms for storage and placed closets in the upper part that can reached by stairs. They also hung sliding doors that can manipulate the space. Enormous sliding panels close off the bedroom at night and create a continuous space during the day. The partition walls in the bathroom are made of glass in order to provide natural illumination.

Cecconi Simone designed various objects specifically for the loft, including the stairs that also serve as a towel bar in the bathroom, the lights, the kitchen cabinets and the bed that features hangers on both sides and drawers on the inside.

This project won a prestigious prize from Ontario's Interior Designers Association.

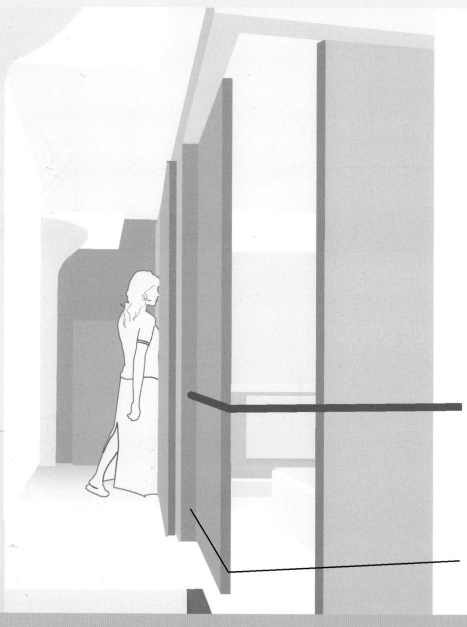

Architects: Cecconi Simone Inc. **Photographs:** Joy von Tiedemann **Location:** Toronto, Canada **Commpletion date:** 1997 **Area:** 623 sq. ft.

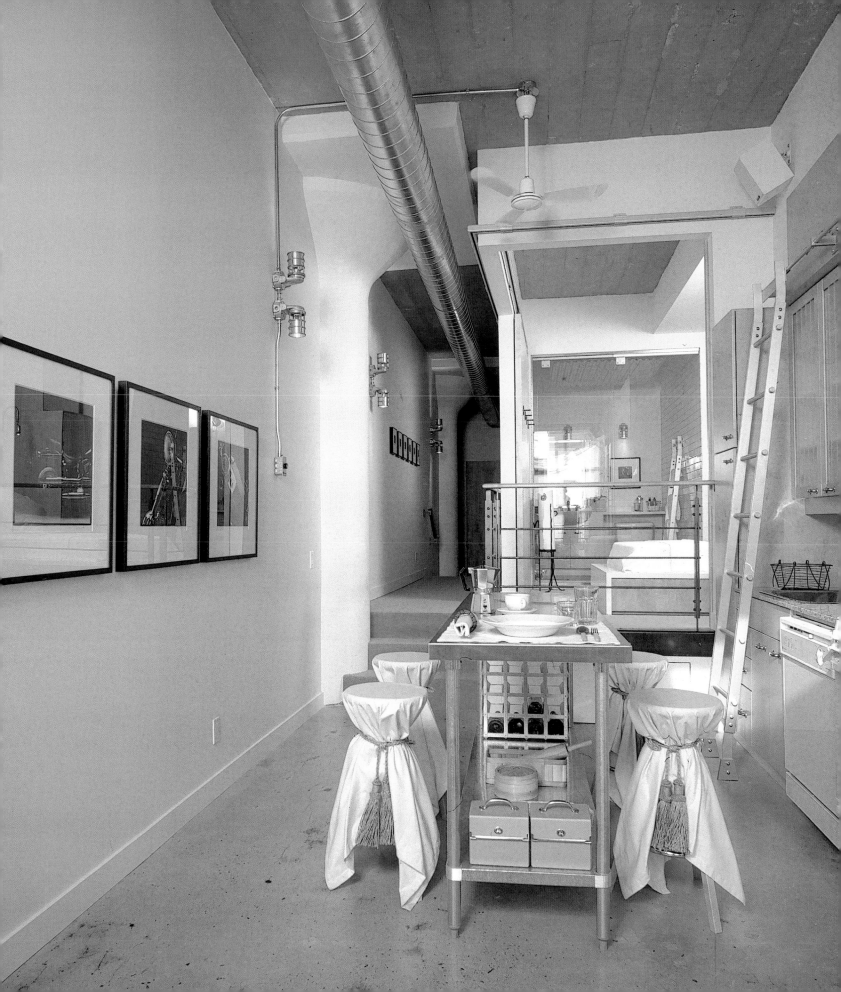

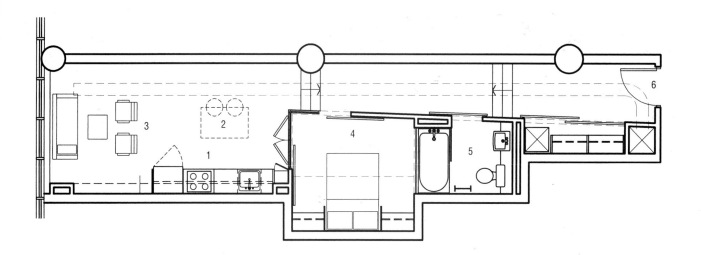

1. Kitchen
2. Dining area
3. Living room
4. Bedroom
5. Bathroom
6. Entryway

THIS PAGE. The service zones are located i
the entryway and the elevated bathroo
and bedroom are situated in the central pa
with views of the kitchen and living roo
Each space is designed to take full advar
tage of natural light.

NEXT PAGE. The project's tone comes fro
the color of the natural materials use
birch wood for the doors and kitche
anodized metal for the stairs and lamps an
steel for the ceiling and parts of the floor.

The upper part of the loft houses several closets and shelving units that can be reached by way of mobile, aluminum stairs with a nautical flair.

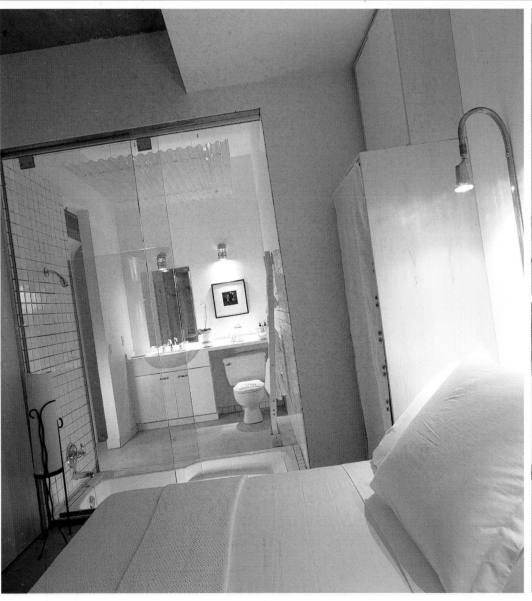

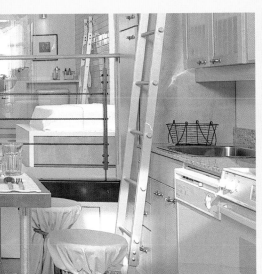

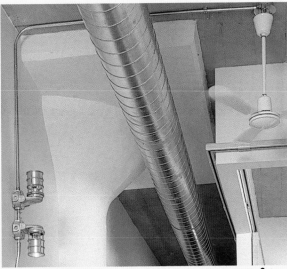

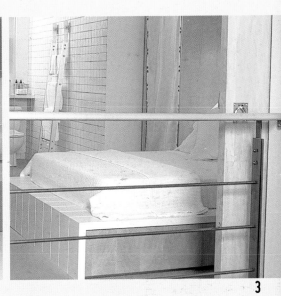

1

2

3

DESIGN SOLUTIONS

1. The continuity between spaces allows the residence to be perceived as a spacious unit. Sliding doors enable the areas that need privacy to be closed off, such as the bedroom and bathroom.

2. The electrical and lighting systems were designed with utmost care since the installations were left exposed to avoid the use of a false ceiling, which formerly occupied the space now used for closets.

3. Cecconi Simone designed the bed, which features hangers on both sides and extra storage space on the inside.

A TRANQUIL OASIS
Claesson Koivisto Rune Arkitektkontor

A young executive commissioned this project for a serene and tranquil home where he can rest and relax when his busy work life permits it. The apartment is located in downtown Stockholm, in a building that features the typical characteristics of constructions built at the end of the 19th Century: hardwood floors and stucco walls.

The architects' first decision was to preserve the spirit of the original construction in the living room and to design a new space for the kitchen, dining room, bedroom and bathroom. To emphasize the contrast between the two zones, they conserved the original white color and painted the new walls and the restored ceiling gray.

They laid out the floor plan in order to make visual communication fluid and to link all of the spaces. The curved wall in the entrance acts as the principal axis and runs along the apartment, delimiting the new spaces on one side and the living room on the other. The second axis, that crosses the entire house, separates the bathroom from the dining room and contains the kitchen cabinets.

Glass screens inserted into the partition walls play a key role in the project's composition: the first two, made of translucent glass, respectively separate the bathroom from the entrance and the kitchen; another transparent one forms part of the wall that defines the bedroom; and the last, an acid-treated mirror, is hung on the bedroom wall to create the optical illusion of spatial continuity.

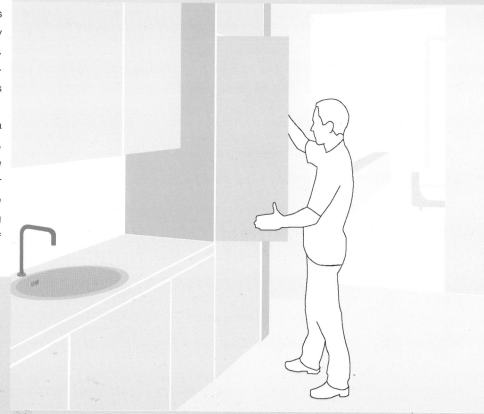

Architects: Claesson Koivisto Rune Arkitektkontor **Photographs:** Patrik Engquist **Location:** Stockholm, Sweden **Completion date:** 1999 **Area:** 699 sq. feet

RIGHT. The drawing depicts the two modules of the residence: the one that houses the original living room and the new zone. The floors are pinewood tinted white, the walls are plastered and painted gray and the furnishings are made of wood and stainless steel.

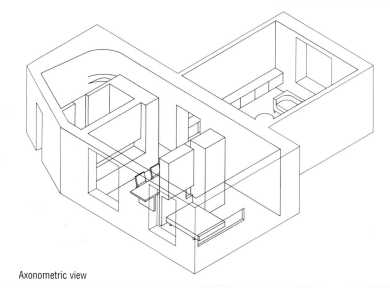

Axonometric view

  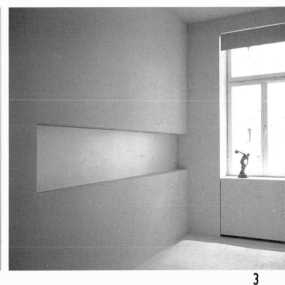

1   2   3

DESIGN SOLUTIONS

1. The living room, which preserves the building's original spirit, and the newly designed area are visually related and share a wall. This continuity amplifies the perception of the residence.

2. The architects painted the new area in the same light gray color to emphasize the project's guiding principles: continuity and aesthetic harmony.

3. Glass inserts in most of the walls permit visual communication between the spaces. An acid-treated mirror in the bedroom virtually duplicates the area.

POLYVALENT APARTMENT
Simon Platt and Rob Dubois

THE plans for this apartment, which belongs to Simon Platt, were drawn up with the aim of conserving the diaphanous quality of the space. It looks out onto one of Barcelona's most attractive squares and was formerly a painter's studio.

The original floor, made of rough-cut tufa, and the vaulted ceilings unify the space, which is an oblong bay articulated into two zones thanks to a mass in the center of the dwelling. This mass, which strategically arranges the space, contains rooms used for different functions: the kitchen, leading to the dinette, the living room, the bathroom, and the master bedroom, with its built-in closets. Thus, the rooms merge together into a space of minimal proportions. The living room and the master bedroom enjoy the greatest surface area, openness and the fine views.

Two balconies open the living room and the dininig area onto the panorama of the square. The rooms are separated from the kitchen by a serving counter which may also be used for quick meals. At the other end of the oblong bay, which looks onto a quiet landscaped patio in the middle of the block, is a bedroom which is open to the rest of the space but can be closed off with sliding doors suspended from the ceiling beams. This mechanism permits the use of the space as an office or a guest room. Thus, this polyvalent apartment serves as a single, diaphanous space or as a three-room dwelling.

The existence of two beams that run from the façades to the staircase creates a play of angles a moment that both increases perspective and gives the entire apartment added interest.

Architects: Simon Platt and Rob Dubois **Photographs:** Eugeni Pons **Location:** Barcelona, Spain **Completion date:** 1999 **Area:** 750 sq. feet

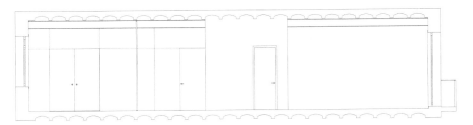

Longitudinal section from the shelves

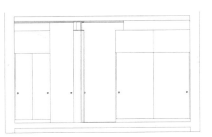

Transversal section

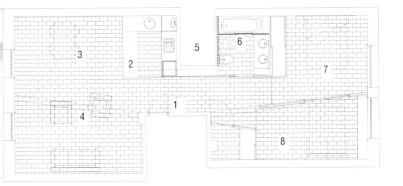

Longitudinal section from the entrance

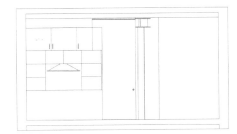

Cross section from the kitchen

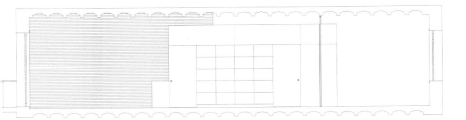

Plan

1. Entrance
2. Kitchen
3. Dinette
4. Living room
5. Interior patio
6. Bathroom
7. Master bedroom
8. Office/guest-room

RIGHT. The main closet juts out into the master bedroom. Wood is the selected material for all the facings and furnishings. Rough-cut tufa covers the floor.

PREVIOUS PAGE. The beams running fro the staircase to the façade establish a dire tion contrasting with the original set-up.

THIS PAGE. Thanks to the ceiling height a the absence of partition walls, the spa feels wider than it really is.

1

2

3

DESIGN SOLUTIONS

1. A piece of furniture placed in the center of the house acts as a pivot point for the rooms: the kitchen, opening onto the living room, the bathroom, and the closets of the master bedroom.

2. The architects made it possible to divide the back part of the apartment using sliding doors suspended from the ceiling. Thus, the main room can be extended or used as another bedroom or studio.

3. Using only those materials and furnishings that are absolutely necessary makes the small area seem move spacious. There are no superfluous objects to disturb the eye as light floods in from outside.

ORGANIC SPACES
Claesson Koivisto Rune Arkitektkontor

THIS project features the downtown Stockholm apartment of an architect who forms part of this Swedish team. Since the client is also one of the firm's designers, the space embodies the group's precepts: continuity between spaces, exquisite constructional details and serene ambiences with sparks of color.

Due to the apartment's small size, 763 square feet, the architects avoided the use of doors, except in the foyer and bathroom. Though the partitions between the spaces run the entire height of the apartment, they do not quite touch the ceiling. This creates a relationship between rooms that enables the house to be perceived as a unit, like a collection of organic spaces.

The communal areas, the living room, dining room, bathroom and kitchen, are located on the first floor. The partition wall that separates the dining room from the living room supports a set of stairs that leads to the upper level, where a small studio and a bedroom are located. The bedroom has access to a terrace with views of the city.

As with most of their projects, the young architects used limited materials in the apartment: light wood for the floors and furniture, a glazed mosaic in the bathroom and kitchen, a wool rug in the private zones and bright colors on some of the walls. Minerals collected in the Arizona desert inspired the project's tonalities. The team, which also specializes in industrial design, combined various furnishings and design objects with pieces of their own creation.

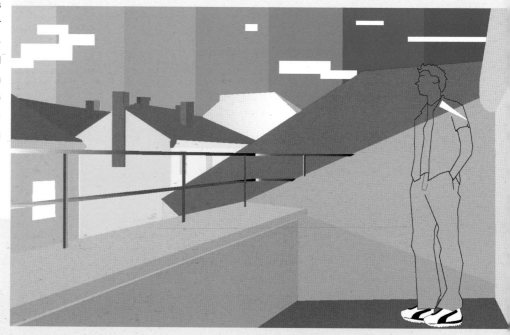

Architects: Claesson Koivisto Rune Arkitektkontor **Photographs:** Patrick Engquist **Location:** Stockholm, Sweden **Completion date:** 2000 **Area:** 763 sq. feet

PREVIOS PAGE. Image of the continuous bench that relates all of the spaces on the first floor. To the right, a detail from the bathroom: the pine wood closet designed by Marten Claesson hides a small, lineal lamp that uniformly illuminates the space.

THIS PAGE. Images of the partitions that separate the spaces. The layout of the walls eliminates the need for doors, maintaining privacy without losing continuity.

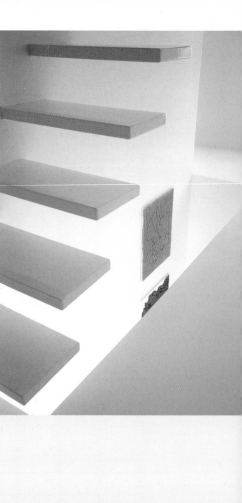

PREVIOUS PAGE. The small studio enjoys abundant natural light thanks to the window that overlooks the landscaped exterior. The client designed the office desk, and Arne Jacobsen created the floor lamp.

THIS PAGE. The bedroom occupies the top floor of an old building, with sloping walls. In order to tone down the lack of useful space, the architects installed windows that run along the wall and continue towards the roof. The windows lift the ceiling and introduce light and views.

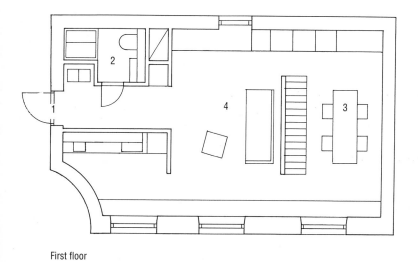

First floor

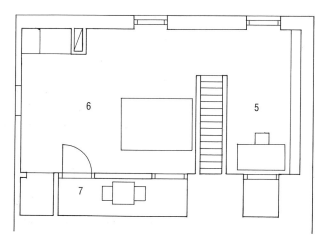

Attic

1. Entrance
2. Bathroom
3. Dining room
4. Living room
5. Studio
6. Bedroom
7. Terrace

  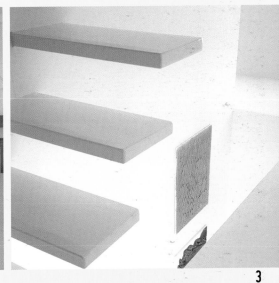

1   2   3

DESIGN SOLUTIONS

1. Closets occupy most of the apartment's interior spaces and are only interrupted by windows or nooks that serve as shelves or tables. The result is an efficient use of space and abundant storage.

2. The windows in the attic façade illuminate the bedroom and make it seem larger.

3. The staircase is supported by a partition wall, which enables it to occupy a very small space.

SUBTLE DISTRIBUTION
Madinabeitia and Barrio

THE reformation of this apartment in Logroño centered around two partition walls that define an open room as the principal space. Distributed around this area are the dwelling's other major volumes: a bathroom, the kitchen and two bedrooms. The living room features white elements that are set off by wood in order to link the apartment's interior to the exterior. Wood is used for the columns, furnishings and room dividers, and helps create a layout with directional concepts and strong, clear lines.

The large glass door that leads to the terrace from the living room changes the natural light into an integrating medium that links the exterior and thus gains additional space for the rest of the dwelling. The wood used in both the terrace and the living room has been treated with natural oils and waxes to resist sun and rain.

The partition walls dividing the kitchen and bedrooms have been used ingeniously as the ideal solution to integrate the oblong space and maximize its suitability for different functions. The subtle flow of light lessens the harsh angles of the columns.

In contrast, the gray tiles of the kitchen floor can be seen as elements that subtly break up the wood-on-white interior of the larger rooms.

Strong lines, light and continuity are distinctive elements in the work by Iñaki Madinabeitia and Araceli Barrio.

Architects: Madinabeitia and Barrio **Photographs:** César San Millán **Location:** Logroño, Spain **Completion date:** 1998 **Area:** 850 sq. feet

THIS PAGE. The vertical board partition shown here, like its hinged counterpart, is pivotal. It closes off the terrace and insulates and shades the dwelling.

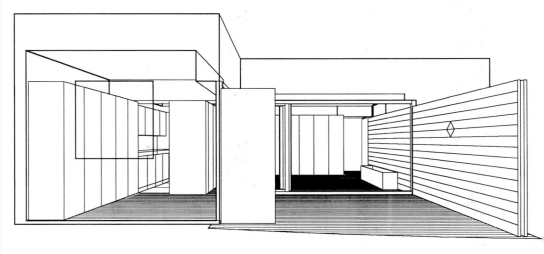

Joint perspectiv

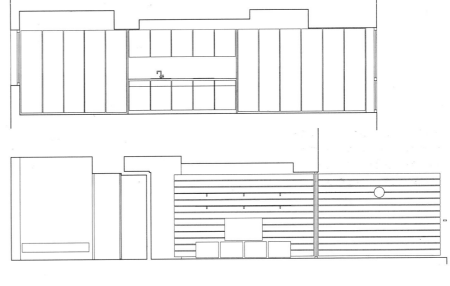

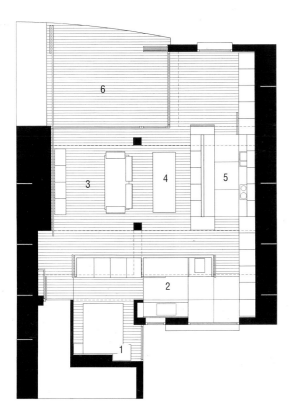

1. Bedroom
2. Bathroom
3. Living room
4. Dining room
5. Kitchen
6. Terrace

LEFT. The layout and furniture create pure, defined lines.

RIGHT. Perspective of the dining room and the fixed partition separating it from the kitchen.

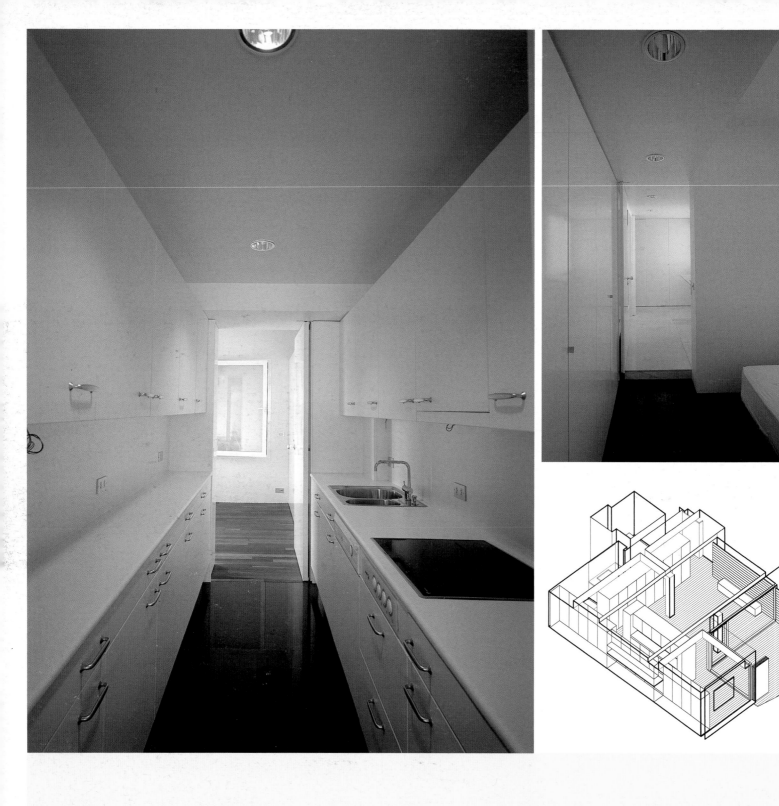

LEFT. The multifunctional kitchen: maximum synthesis and practicality.
RIGHT. Detail of the bedroom.

1

2

3

DESIGN SOLUTIONS

1. The terrace and the living room are two spaces virtually integrated by a screen that simultaneously connects and differentiates them.

2. The adapted screen provides ample space for the dining room and kitchen.

3. To maximize the view of the horizon from the terrace, the old wall separating terrace and balcony was knocked down and replaced with a large pane of glass.

DIAPHANOUS CONTINUITY
A-cero Architects

THE first glimpse of this apartment showed a narrow entranceway into a space that was cut up and poorly lit. The principal objective was to refurbish the attic and create a luminous home. To achieve this end, the architects removed all of the partitions, replaced the existing woodwork and brought in natural light and views.

The existing mezzanine was used, but modified lightly in the area around the staircase. Eliminations were also made in the hall to alleviate the feeling of narrowness in the entranceway. The column that supported the mezzanine was replaced by a tension rod, which decreassed the perception of heaviness.

The program permitted minimal reduction of the closed spaces (basically the bathrooms), and an attempt was made to unify the remaining space, including the kitchen, the dining room and the living room. The large continuous and diaphanous surface area divides domestic functions by way of small differences in levels or the changing nature of the floor or the ceiling. All the small residual spaces are used for storage: one in the entrance, another for the pantry and kitchen sink, still another for luggage, and one used to house the washer, dryer and cleaning materials.

Stairs recessed in the wall lead to an upper level that includes the bedroom, a bathroom and a dressing room.

The facings meet the criterion of austerity that controls the whole. White paint was used on walls, floor, and ceilings, except for the partitions in the bathrooms, which are glass and create a totally waterproof surface with almost no joints.

The complete furnishings were designed as part of the project, from the picture frames to the armchairs. Outstanding in their complexity are the piece in the kitchen, which contains all the appliances, and the bathroom elements.

Architects: A-cero Architects **Photographs:** Juan Rodríguez **Location:** La Coruña, Spain **Completion date:** 1999 **Area:** 860 sq. feet

THIS PAGE. Various perspectives of the dining room and the living room, where one can appreciate the different levels marking off the various domestic functions. The levels eliminate the need to raise more walls. At the back, the long windows offer magnificent city views.

NEXT PAGE. View of the upper level from the living room. This second level is built over the kitchen and the dining room and contains the bedroom, a dressing room and a bathroom.

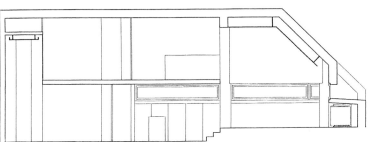

Sections from the entry

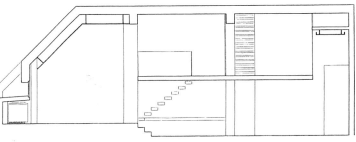

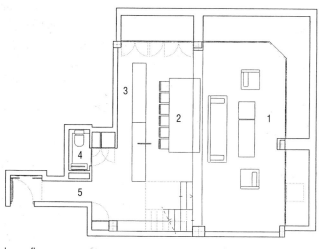
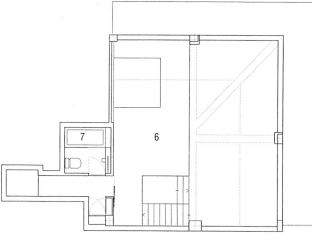

1. Living room
2. Dining room
3. Kitchen
4. Toilet
5. Entrance
6. Bedroom
7. Bathroom

Lower floor

Upper floor

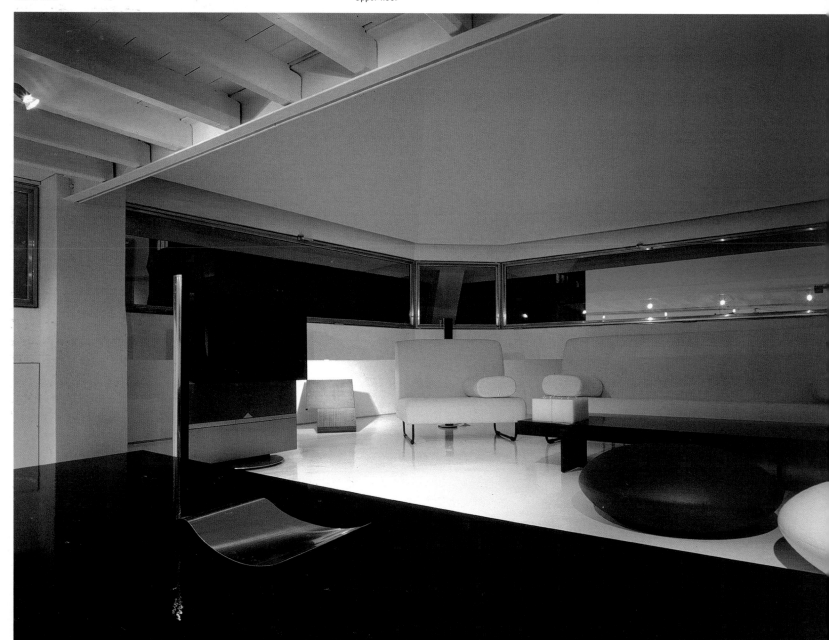

PREVIOUS PAGE. The architects designed all the wood and stainless steel furniture, which was made by carpenters.

THIS PAGE. Detail of the bedroom. The furnishings and décor are minimized at the client's request. The artificial lighting is concealed behind a double wall to avoid use of lamps that would clutter the space.

THIS PAGE. The bathroom sink was designed by the project's young architects. It is made of an oblong sheet-metal box perforated on top and secured to the wall with nails. The faucet is long and elegant and has a small rectangular opening for water flow, regulated by a foot-operated control in the floor.

1

2

3

DESIGN SOLUTIONS

1. There are recessed cabinets concealed throughout the house. Although it is difficult to see them in the photos, they are of great practical use to the owner, who receives many visitors and wants an orderly space that can be cleaned quickly.

2. The indirect relationship between the rooms brings out the sensation of space. The partition wall in the bedroom is less than 5 feet high and lets light flow in freely. It is also slightly inclined to give the bedroom greater volume.

3. The stairs were minimized when the use of boundary partitions was eliminated. In this way, the staircase occupies only a limited space in both lower and upper levels.

A REFORMED STABLE
Haehndel and Coll

THIS old house is located in the center of Sant Cugat del Vallès, in the province of Barcelona. The building originally housed a stable that was constructed in the same style as most of the pueblo's older homes. The space later became a dressmaker's workshop.

After years of vacancy and disuse, two young couples restored the space according to their housing requirements. On the ground floor, the architects tried to preserve the original distribution that is so typical of the village's early homes, including the kitchen in the entryway. To amplify the foyer and make it more interesting, the architects substituted the dividing wall of the kitchen with a bar. The area that once housed the stable, and then the dressmaker's workshop, is now the living room, which preserves the original, vaulted Catalan herringbone ceiling. The living area also contains a fireplace with simple lines and a loft bed that comfortably converts it into sleeping quarters.

Light is the focus in the studio thanks to a glass ceiling and a glass door that opens onto a small garden with a Japanese feel. For both the interior and the exterior space, the architects chose a wooden floor that unifies the house and gives it a feeling of length and spaciousness. Another highlight of the project is its two distinct atmospheres. The interior combines antique elements with simple lines, while the exterior is much more modern.

Architects: Haehndel and Coll **Photographs:** David Cardelús **Location:** Sant Cugat del Vallès, Spain **Completion date:** 2000 **Area:** 860 sq. feet

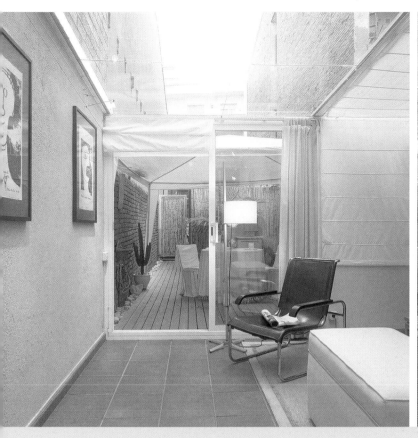

THIS PAGE. Views of the work area located in the gallery. The architects hung cloth awnings on the glass roof that work like interior blinds, shielding the space from the sun's rays in the summer and absorbing the cold in the winter. The doors are also made of glass and blur the distinction between the inside and the outside.

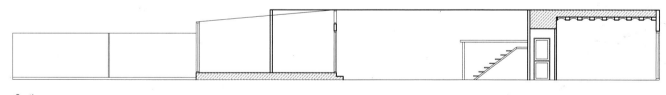

Section

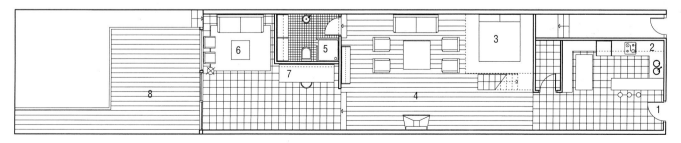

Floor plan

1. Entry
2. Kitchen
3. Loft bed
4. Living room
5. Bathroom
6. Gallery
7. Office
8. Terrace

THIS PAGE. All the domestic functions are contained in a unique space that takes full advantage of every nook. The dining area, for example, is located in a corner, and a loft bed converts the living room into sleeping quarters.

1

2

3

DESIGN SOLUTIONS

1. The fluid relationship between the interior space and the exterior terrace conveys a feeling of spaciousness.

2. Thanks to the high ceilings, the bed is set up as a sleeping loft. This frees the space underneath to be used for something else; in this case, a piano. The original vaulted ceiling gives the house warmth.

3. The gallery, used as a work area, features glass ceilings that amplify the virtual area. Cloth awnings filter the sun's light and prevent a glare.

INDUSTRIAL PAST
Olli Sarlin and Marja Sopanen

THIS residence is located on the ground floor of an old textile factory. The red brick building was constructed in 1928 in the historic center of Helsinki and was renovated into apartments several years ago.

The ground floor originally served as the factory office and was later converted into a commercial space. In the Eighties, all the beams were covered with a false ceiling and various floorings were added.

This project's objective was to uncover the factory's antique structure and convert it into an apartment with open space. All the vertical partitions were eliminated and the false ceilings removed. The steel beams were restored and some parts of the ceiling were painted with tinted glue. The brick, once cleaned, was rejoined using a mixture of beer and agglutinating agent.

The wooden tie beams were reused as supports for the varnished pine floor that was installed on top of the original one. The architects improved the floor's acoustics by adding cellulose, which absorbs sound reverberations and cuts down on the noise made by walking. The architects left a space between the wooden floorboards and the walls, in which to insert the heating pipes. This technique avoided the need to cut channels for the pipes in the walls.

The L-shaped residence is organized so that the bathroom and kitchen occupy the smaller part of the apartment. A large living room and bedroom are located in the more spacious area that covers the building's entire dimensions.

The bathroom is housed in a new covered structure made of plywood that also contains, on one end, the oven and the kitchen cabinets. This new volume does not reach the ceiling in order to leave a space that can be used for storage.

Architects: Olli Sarlin and Marja Sopanen **Photographs:** Arno de la Chapelle **Location:** Helsinki, Finland **Completion date:** 1997 **Area:** 915 sq. feet

THIS PAGE. All the elements that make up the residence are mobile and allow different divisions of the space. Furthermore, the architects used various recycled materials such as antique cabinets from a hospital, secondhand refrigerators and kitchen cabinetry that was originally designed for industrial use.

1

2

3

DESIGN SOLUTIONS

1. The large living room and bedroom are separated by a cabinet on wheels that can be moved. The bed is also mobile, making the entire distribution variable.

2. The bathroom occupies a volume that was constructed in the original surroundings. The volume does not reach the ceiling, leaving a space above that can be used as a small warehouse. The architects took full advantage of every space.

3. A new plywood volume was built to house the bathroom on the interior and kitchen cabinets and the oven on the exterior. This strategy unites various domestic functions in a minimal space.

INDUSTRIAL LOFTS

Cecconi Simone Inc.

CANDEM LOFTS is a new residential building of lofts located in downtown Toronto. Once an apartment block, the building now houses 55 units between 591 and 1,204 square feet, plus a floor of underground parking.

From the beginning of the project, the building served as the architectural inspiration for the lofts and their design. The possibility of creating varied and imaginative residential spaces in the building added value to the structure.

Cecconi Simone Inc. designed both the loft units and the communal zones, including the hallways and foyer of the preexisting building. The suites bring together the best elements of the loft style: spacious areas for living and dining, high ceilings and windows that look out on the city. In a building just in front of the site, the architectural firm created a model unit to facilitate the sales process before construction had even begun.

All the lofts share a common architectural characteristic: exposed reinforced concrete walls that act as a reference element and provoke contrasts in the interior ambience of each residence.

Architects: Cecconi Simone Inc. **Photographs:** Joy von Tiedemann **Location:** Toronto, Canada **Completion date:** 1999 **Area:** 915 sq. feet

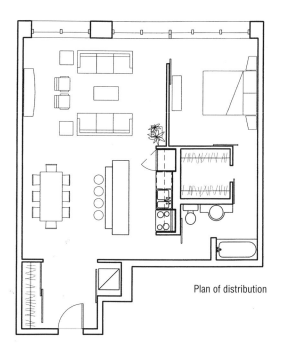

Plan of distribution

ABOVE. The coldness of the concrete is softened by the use of materials like wood, fabrics and decorative elements such as candles. The heterogeneous composition reflects the neighborhood's boisterous character.

TO THE RIGHT. Cecconi Simone Inc. also designed the bedroom furniture.

PREVIOUS PAGE. The open kitchen, breakfast bar and industrial lighting are the elements that characterize the design of the space.

1

2

3

DESIGN SOLUTIONS

1. The false ceilings were eliminated in order to give the small units a feeling of spaciousness. As a result, the electrical installations and the structural system are left exposed.

2. In order to visually relate the spaces, the architects avoided vertical partitions. The structural columns seem to compartmentalize the adjoining spaces.

3. All the rooms preserve the building's industrial spirit. This stylistic continuity gives the space the feeling of being unique and indissoluble.

TRANSLUCENT STAIRCASE
W. Camagna, M. Camoletto and A. Marcante

THE commission was to remodel a dark, empty attic on the fourth floor of an 18th Century building in the baroque center of Turin, Italy. The clients, a young couple who are enterprising business people, wanted to make the most out of the apartment's small space. They chose to organize it on two levels with a total surface area of just under 960 square feet.

The result is orderly living quarters with a vertical layout of the rooms and the domestic functions. On the lower level they put two bedrooms with their respective bathrooms and a storage closet. The upper level contains space for daytime activities: the kitchen, a pantry, the living room and the dining room. All these spaces, except that used for storage, are integrated into one single unit. This increases the perception of the house's size. The multivalent apartment is, moreover, lighted by a large window that keys open by way of an electrical device to provide light for the lower level.

The staircase joining the two levels is the project's nerve center. It connects both levels and increases natural light flow. The metal frame holds up, in the first flight, birch steps without risers; the second flight features steps of sand-blasted glass. The whole element is supported by a double-height partition that includes a birch bookcase.

The choice of work materials brings out the connection between the spaces, for example, the use of glass partitions in place of walls. The heavy wooden beams used in the original construction have also been replaced by light metal pieces that increase usable height.

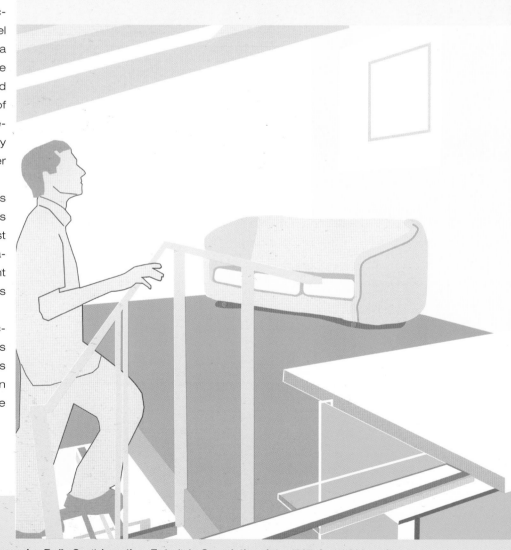

Architects: W. Camagna, M. Camoletto and A. Marcante **Photographs:** Emilio Conti **Location:** Turin, Italy **Completion date:** 1997 **Area:** 960 sq. feet

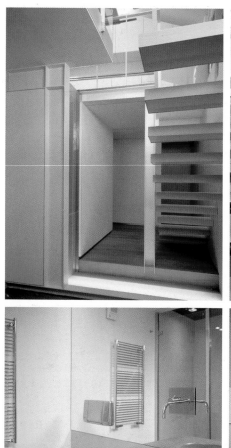

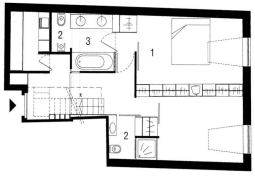
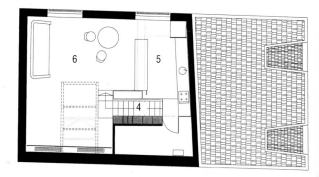

THIS PAGE. Details of different parts of the apartment. In spite of the limited surface area, the plan serves all necessary domestic functions and there is even a space for two complementary bathrooms.

NEXT PAGE. View of the staircase. The double-height wall includes a bookcase which is reached from the steps.

Lower level

1. Bedroom
2. Toilet
3. Bathroom

Upper level

4. Stairway
5. Kitchen
6. Living room

1   2   3

DESIGN SOLUTIONS

1. The absence of risers in the steps and the materials used in the staircase turn it into an ethereal element that does not interrupt the fluidity of the space.

2. What was once a dark attic became a light-filled living space thanks to the installation of large windows in the roof.

3. The upper level, which contains the kitchen, the dining room, and the living room, was designed to be perceived as an attic that does not take up the whole condominium. The transparent material of the handrails makes it possible to view full dimensions of the two levels from the attic.

MINIMALIST ATTIC APARTMENT

Marco Savorelli

THIS project entailed the restoration of an attic apartment in the historic center of Milan. The 968 square foot space was transformed into a modern, sophisticated and elegant loft.

The architect disregarded the space's former layout and focused on a new distribution plan. The general concept was to integrate all the rooms into a single space, thus avoiding doors and interior partitions. The choice of only one type of flooring, dark hardwood, also contributes to a feeling of unity. The floor's tone contrasts with the clean, white walls and inclined ceilings.

The client and architect worked closely together throughout the entire project and opted to start from scratch. They followed abstract concepts that enabled the residence to evolve during the renovation process. The property's old functions were replaced with useful, simple and innovative forms.

Keeping in mind the sloped ceilings, the architect created a principal axis of circulation in the center of the dwelling, where the ceilings are the highest. The spaces for activities related to leisure or relaxation were constructed in the perimeter.

The service areas, like the bathroom, the kitchen and the cabinets, are monolithic volumes. When reduced to simple forms, they become works of plastic arts that give new meaning to the spatial perception. Both functional and eccentric, the volumes lack instrumental validity and teeter on the edge of irony and provocation.

Since this attic apartment is a clear succession of spaces with no defined frontiers, the entryway becomes the living room and the bedroom melts into the bathroom and the kitchen, which is the apartment's neurological center.

Architect: Marco Savorelli **Photographs:** Matteo Piazza **Location:** Milan, Italy **Completion date:** 1999 **Area:** 960 sq. ft.

THIS PAGE. The bathtub, a quadrilateral stone, and the shower, made of glass, are located in the bedroom. Both elements appear as independent volumes that are visually connected to the rest of the room. Only the toilet is separated by a partition wall. Since there are no vertical partitions that delimit the domestic areas, the architect and client chose a restricted palette for materials in order to unify the atmosphere of the apartment.

1. Living room
2. Kitchen
3. Toilet
4. Bathtub
5. Bedroom
6. Shower
7. Living area

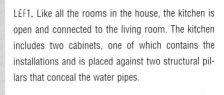

LEFT. Like all the rooms in the house, the kitchen is open and connected to the living room. The kitchen includes two cabinets, one of which contains the installations and is placed against two structural pillars that conceal the water pipes.

RIGHT. The sofas were designed according to the project's guidelines: floating bodies of wood with cushions in a light fabric that combines with the overall tone of the surroundings. The attic's large, inclined windows are reminiscent of days gone by and allow abundant natural light to enter the space. The artificial lighting consists of a system of recessed cans that are placed discreetly throughout the loft.

1

2

3

DESIGN SOLUTIONS

1. Since only one person resides in the apartment, there were no privacy issues. This made it possible for the bathtub and shower to form part of the bedroom, eliminating the need for vertical partitions that would break up the space

2. The kitchen occupies the central zone of the apartment. The refrigerator is placed in a space between structural columns, and a kitchen cabinet is also used as a countertop for eating.

3. The attic's sloped ceilings are interspersed with large windows that let in natural light and prevent the ceiling's limited height from being uncomfortable.

LUMINOUS CONTINUITY
Christophe Pillet

THIS apartment by prestigious designer Christophe Pillet demonstrates his skill in making the most of spaces with limited dimensions. The project is located in an old office in Paris that was renovated as a residence. Thanks to several large windows, the locale enjoys abundant natural light which Pillet played up in order to compensate for the apartment's limited size.

In a small home, every corner must be versatile and able to house distinct functions. For this reason, Pillet opted to avoid hallways, since they are unnecessary when the spaces are linked and continual. He also eliminated partition walls, except for one that defines the bathroom and a sliding door that gives the bedroom privacy. This strategy converts the house into a large, luminous, multifunctional room that seems whole from every angle.

The kitchen, which is located in front of the entrance, includes two fronted cabinets that are built into the lateral wall and that contain all of the installations. The dining room and the living room occupy the large rectangular space, and the bedroom and bathroom are situated next to the other lateral wall. The two façades have no installations and can thus accommodate the large windows without being conditioned by structural prerequisites.

The apartment is painted white to emphasize light, and several decorative objects lend a splash of color to the uniform ambience. Pillet designed some of the furnishings himself.

Architect: Christophe Pillet **Photographs:** Jean François Jaussaud **Location:** Paris, France **Completion date:** 2000 **Area:** 960 sq. feet

RIGHT. Image of the living room with the kitchen in the background. Since two fronted modules are hung in the kitchen, there was no need to close off the space laterally. As a result, the architect achieved a certain functional isolation and easy accessibility.

NEXT PAGE. Details of the apartment's furnishings and decorations, including pieces by famous designers, such as the dining chairs by Charles and Ray Eames.

1. Entrance
2. Kitchen
3. Dining room
4. Living room
5. Bedroom
6. Bathroom

1   2   3

DESIGN SOLUTIONS

1. Light plays a determining role in the perception of the spaces and makes them seem larger. The use of the color white to emphasize luminosity is a well-known and effective strategy.

2. The layout of the spaces did not require hallways, avoiding the unnecessary use of the apartment's valued space.

3. The 22 square foot kitchen was designed as a piece of furniture to hold all of the installations. Despite its small area, the kitchen is very practical.

FLOATING ISLAND
Voon Wong

THE architect Voon Yee Wong refurbished a small apartment in South London to use as his home and studio. The project, located in the second story of a Victorian building formerly used as a school, increased both light and space. The area that Voon had to work with was an empty 13-foot cube with access to the outside by way of two bay windows.

In order to take full advantage of the vertical height, the designer approached the plan with the idea of inserting a mass in space—to create an island floating in emptiness. His first step was to build a frame to support the mezzanine and organize the areas. This established a double-height zone next to the main front, where the living room was installed.

To increase the amount of light, the architect reduced the number of room dividers to what he considered the bare minimum, closing off only the bathrooms.

On the first floor, the living room, dining room, and kitchen flow into each other in a continuous and open discourse. The kitchen is a box that has been suspended off the ground from the mezzanine. It contains a range and cabinets and can be closed off with white sliding panels. Facing the kitchen, and built into one of the walls, is a refrigerator installed in a white wood container that protrudes into the living room to emphasize the impression of visual continuity.

A stairway beside the entrance leads to the upper story, and provides independent access to the bedroom and the studio. Privacy is conferred here without the use of doors. The two spaces effectively "grow into" the living room and thus share the abundant light. The bedroom also does this, but by way of a glass screen, and the studio uses a half-height partition to incorporate Voon's work table.

Architect: Voon Yee Wong **Photographs:** Henry Wilson **Location:** London, UK **Completain date:** 1998 **Area:** 960 sq. feet

THIS PAGE. Details of the finishes and decorative elements. The ceilings, walls, doors, and built-in furniture are white; the floor has been painted a glossy dark gray. Intense color on some walls sets off the soft tones.

NEXT PAGE. The dining room, located beneath the mezzanine, defines itself by its furniture: a tabled designed by the architect, stools and a large bench built into a nook.

1. Living room
2. Kitchen
3. Entrance
4. Dining room
5. Bathroom
6. Toilet
7. Bedroom
8. Studio

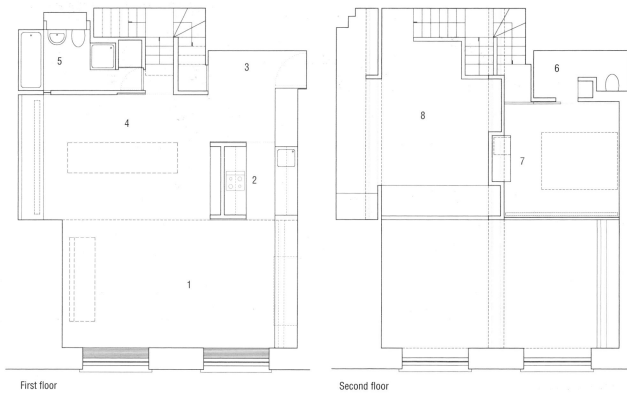

First floor

Second floor

THIS PAGE. Lighting and other installations are located under the floor and inside the walls to avoid cluttering the space.

NEXT PAGE. Photos showing different storage ideas: the bedroom wardrobe, a shelf on the first floor and a recessed shelf in the studio.

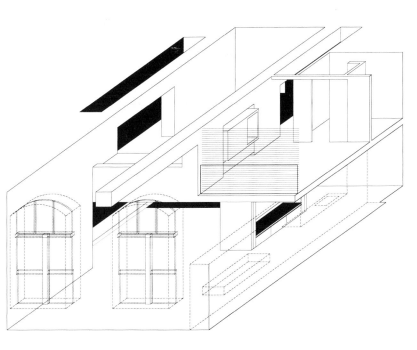

Axonometric perspective

1   2   3

DESIGN SOLUTIONS

1. The architect takes full advantage of the mezzanine's small space. It contains his bedroom and his studio, which are reached independently by way of a stairway that divides at the top.

2. To increase the feel of openness, the partition walls were removed. Only the bathrooms have fixed partitions. The house thus takes on the look of a large, multi-functional space.

3. Light-colored materials, some painted white, provide maximum reflection of light from the only two windows. Glass panels on the mezzanine's railing bring light to the bedroom.

SPIRAL TRIP
Satoshi Okada

THIS house is located in a city near Tokyo. The lot's location, 4.9 feet above street level, recalls the past of this zone, which is made up of a sort of series of hills that are disappearing rapidly due to the hegemony of the metropolis.

The house is arranged on multiple plains that reflect the topography of the surroundings. By way of a spiral string, the staircase relates all the levels, each of which has a distinct feel, defines a different dimension, and generates a continuity between the last room and the next. The systematic composition of the floors is supported on the bearing walls around the building. Thus, some partition walls could be removed because they are not structurally necessary: this gives the rooms a borderless effect. Without the usual partition walls, the relationship between volumes is much more direct.

The divisions between spaces are reminiscent of the paper-and-wood panels of traditional Japanese architecture, like the kekkai – elements that work like ambiguous partitions. In this project, the kekkai have been modernized and made into separating instruments of a changing nature. In some rooms, the kekkai are now pieces of furniture, and in the staircase they are represented by a large folding panel to mark off zones. In other cases the kekkai act as an interior partition and in others these serve as dining table for guests or a waiting bench outside the bathroom.

The building's apertures do not follow an ordered composite rhythm, but respond to the demands of the terrain or the need to offer given views of the garden. There are also interior swivel windows that relate different zones at different times of the day.

Architect: Satoshi Okada **Photographs:** Hiroyuki Hirai **Location:** Kawasaki, Japan **Date of construction:** 1999 **Area:** 970 sq. feet

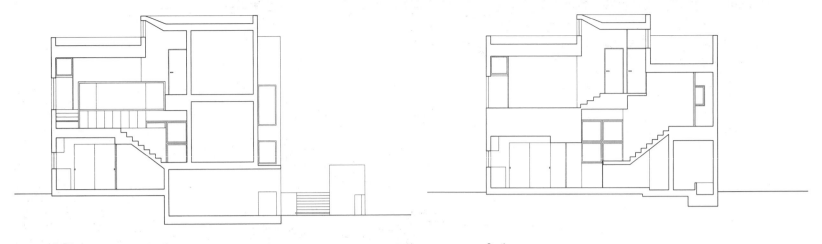

Section

Section

PREVIOUS PAGE. The sections show how the skylights allow for sunlight to penetrate the north part of the house. The stacked arrangement of the dwellings means an interruption in the floors that allows light to reach to the first level.

THIS PAGE. The staircase that joins the rooms of the house is equipped with cabinets. The doors of each compartment correspond to a step and when these are open, they form a unique sculptural element.

1. Entrance
2. Hallway
3. Living room
4. Bedroom
5. Tatami room
6. Living room
7. Kitchen
8. Dining room
9. Bedroom
10. Bedroom
11. Balcony

First floor

Second floor

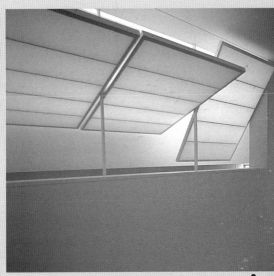

1   2   3

DESIGN SOLUTIONS

1. One of the space-gaining strategies was to place cupboards under the stairway. Each step corresponds to a storage unit, whose size progressively grows in capacity with the ascent of the stairs.

2. The intense relationship with the exterior increases the sensation of space since the inside of the house is close to the garden. Some windows are transparent, others translucent, and although the latter provide no exterior views, they do let in abundant natural light.

3. The swivel panels relate the spaces of the different levels. When privacy is required, it is simply a question of turning the panels to the horizontal position.

TRANSLUCENT COLOR
John Cockings Architects

THIS project is located on a small lot with a garden in a charming neighborhood of Sydney. The assignment entailed converting an existing, deteriorated construction into a home for one person. The spaces on the first floor were dark and humid, the patio was neglected and the layout was impractical.

The architects's objective was to restore the house by placing the living room, kitchen and dining room on the first floor and the bathroom and a dressing room on the second floor. The idea was to create a versatile, light space on the ground floor that would open onto the exterior.

Since the lot measures only 511 square feet and is surrounded by the balconies and terraces of the adjoining buildings, the architects decided to focus on views of the garden and the surrounding trees, in order to avoid visual contact with the neighbors. The priority was to ensure privacy for the residence without closing off the spaces. As a solution, the architects selected glass for the façade leading onto the patio, and installed only one translucent window and a skylight on the upper level.

Since space is so limited, the domestic functions overlap: the kitchen counter becomes a table and the dining room acts as a hallway between the two parts of the living room and becomes a second bedroom when there are guests. The use of glass in this zone opens the room onto the small garden, which becomes an integral part of the residence.

Thanks to the clever layout of the small, related spaces and the lively colors of the glass façade, the designers have managed to create a bright, sophisticated home with a confident air.

Architects: John Cockings Architects **Photographs:** Bratt Boardman **Localition:** Sydney, Australia **Completion date:** 1999 **Area:** 970 sq. feet

1   2   3

DESIGN SOLUTION

1. The architects placed skylights in strategic points to bring light and garden views to the corners that need it most.

2. The house opens onto a patio by way of a glass façade that offers abundant natural light. The residence maintains its privacy thanks to a surrounding wall that separates it from the noise of the city.

3. Despite its reduced dimensions, the interior is comfortable and warm. The use of glass guarantees that all communal spaces are luminous.

3-D EXPANSION
Atelier Suda

THE scarcity of space for building in Japan has meant the disorderly and random growth of the big city suburbs. Yet, thanks to architects like Misuhiro Suda, some interventions not only take advantage of space limitations, they actually turn them into seminal buildings that reorient the area, either architecturally or by way of example for new projects.

The commission required the design of a one-family house on a plot of only 344 square feet located in the Shitamachi neighborhood, traditionally occupied by artisans and artists. In this zone one finds one of the city's most emblematic temples. And owing to the music festivals held there, the neighborhood breathes an exciting and rarefied atmosphere that at times means a kind of urbanistic disorderliness. The dwelling meets functional requirements and also acts like a small oasis in the architectural chaos.

Main objective: clients and designers both wanted to create a ventilated domestic space to deal with the humidity and high temperatures that come with Tokyo's summers. The strategy put to work was to leave a vacuum that connects the living room and the dining room on the ground floor and the bedroom with the studio upstairs. This continuous space moves upward through the whole house and receives the natural light of skylights which open up to add more ventilation.

The staircase that connects the floors was constructed in the center of one of the façades to minimize walkways and avoid unused nooks. Thus all available space plays a role.

Partition walls and dividers are almost unnecessary owing to the staggering of the floors. Furniture was arranged to divide the space into rooms in some cases. These pieces are also used for storage.

Architects: Atelier Suda **Photographs:** Nobuhiro Okamura **Location:** Tokyo, Japan **Completion date:** 1998 **Area:** 980 sq. feet

THIS PAGE. To maintain continuity between spaces and to underline the visual link between rooms, the staircase was designed without risers. The steps bracket on one of the walls and on a junk-storage area.

1. Tatami room
2. Garage
3. Entrance
4. Dining room
5. Living room
6. Kitchen
7. Bathroom
8. Studio
9. Bedroom
10. Balcony

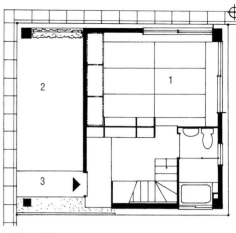

Ground floor

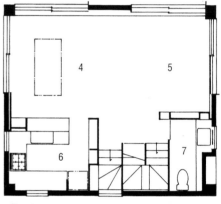

First floor

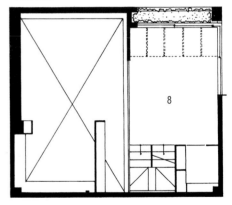

Second floor

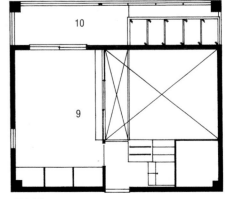

Third floor

1   2   3

DESIGN SOLUTIONS

1. To eliminate halls or unnecessary routes, the staircase was placed in the center of one of the façades. Thus, the route from the entranceway to the different rooms is always shorter.

2. The rooms are not partitioned off conventionally. Elimination of dividers cuts costs and reorganizes space. Pieces of furniture were occasionally used to mark out domestic functions.

3. The placement of rooms that do not take up the whole plan provides a vertical communication that offers continuity to the program's development.

LUMINOUS WALL
Claudio Lazzarini & Carl Pickering

THIS project, created by merging two flats separated by a bearing wall, is located on the 14th floor of the Mirabeau skyscraper.

The client is a businessman who spends part of the week in Montecarlo and usually dines out. The dwelling was therefore conceived as a suite with a terrace to enjoy delightful breakfasts and aperitifs at dusk.

The principal objective was to create a unique, continuous and fluid space in which to enjoy the magnificent views of the sea. To achieve this end, the loading wall that divides the apartment lengthwise was dematerialized by placing mirrors, glass shapes and stainless steel apertures that appear to pass from one side to another.

The bathroom, kitchen and cupboards were conceived as independent units installed as part of this unique space. The terrace, designed like the deck of a ship, is an integral part of the interior. It allows the interior to expand and flow outdoors. The daylight plays with the color of the glazed objects, intensifying and diversifying the effects of the lamps around the apartment.

The light glass boxes on the walls take on an array of tones as the colors filter through them. The partitions have wheels on the bottom and can be moved. The hinged panels were designed to be left open, in order to create numerous perspectives and to offer different ways of dividing up the space.

The bathroom joins onto the bedroom. The shower is behind the bed and the glass screen makes it possible to shower looking at the sea. The shiny surfaces and the transparent glass and mirrors form a mirage of reflections that both cancel out and intensify the artificial light sources, boosting the daylight's impact. The architects also designed some of the furniture in the apartment: the tables, bed and kitchen cabinets. The sofa is from Antonio Citterio and the light fixtures from Kreon.

Architects: Claudio Lazzarini & Carl Pickering **Photographs:** Matteo Piazza **Location:** Montecarlo, Monaco **Completion date:** 1998 **Floor space:** 1,000 sq. ft.

1. Bedroom
2. Living area
3. Kitchen
4. Bathroom
5. Balcony

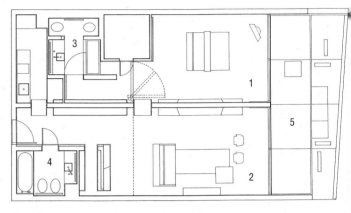

Floor plan

0 ____ 5

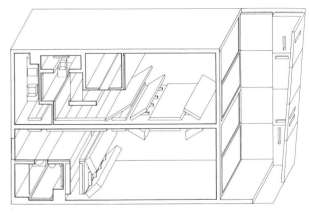

Perspective

PREVIOUS PAGE. The window occupying the upper part of the façade affords unique views of the Bay of Monte Carlo. It also allows abundant light to enter.

TOP. The project consisted of two apartments divided by a load-bearing wall which was opened up to connect the living area and bedroom. This opening eliminated the original, heavy partition and visually connects the different rooms in the house.

BOTTOM. The minimalist finish of the construction materials contrasts with the sophisticated furnishings. The white of the walls and the transparency of the cabinets contrast with the striking colors of the decorative objects.

TOP. One of the most important aspects of the project is the treatment of light: the natural light that filters through the large windows mixes with carefully-designed, artificial illumination to create multiple reflections with the mirrors and polished finishes.

BOTTOM. The bedroom has direct access to the balcony and enjoys sea views. The exterior was treated with the same finishes so that it blends with the bedroom and living area.

NEXT PAGE. The main objective of the project was to create spatial continuity which, due to the reflections, is sometimes just apparent fluidity. These illusions heighten the perception of the whole.

THIS PAGE. Color plays a major role in every room in the apartment. In the living area a few colored objects stand out against the predominant white. In the kitchen, the dark marble makes the sink and refrigerator shine.

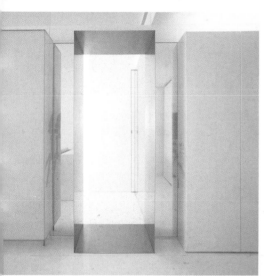

DESIGN SOLUTIONS

1. To achieve greater fluidity between spaces, gaps were opened in the partitions and mirrors were used to reflect different rooms.

2. Movable cabinets make it possible to compartmentalize open-plan space. Their internal lighting and translucent doors make these containers multicolored lamps.

3. The polished, shiny finishes of the different surfaces allow light to reach the farthest nooks and crannies. The reflections also create many optical illusions.

A-cero architects

La Coruña, Spain
Phone 34 981 154 178
Fax 34 981 154 565
a-cero@jet.es
www.a-cero.com

Atelier Suda

Tokyo, Japan
Phone/Fax 81 3 3401 8898

W. Camagna, M. Camoletto and A. Marcante

Turin, Italy
Phone 39 329 229 90 50
Fax 39 011 248 75 91
uda@nevib.it

Claesson Koivisto Rune Arkitektkontor

Stockholm, Sweden
Phone 46 86 44 58 63
Fax 46 86 44 58 83
arkitektkontor@clesson-koivisto-rune.se
www.scandinaviandesign.com/claesson-koivisto-rune

Cecconi Simone Inc.

Toronto, Canada
Phone 1 416 588 59 00
Fax 1 416 588 74 24
info@cecconisimone.com

Eichinger oder Knechtl

Vienna, Austria
Phone 43 1 535 54 240
Fax 43 1 535 40 39
desk@eok.at

Ricardo Flores and Eva Prats

Barcelona, Spain
Phone 34 93 268 43 65
flores-prats@coac.net

Joseph Giovannini Associates

New York, US
Phone 1 1212 297 1850
Fax 1 1212 297 0980

Dorothee Haehndel and Pau Coll

Sant Cugat del Vallès, Barcelona, Spain
Phone 34 93 589 78 58